MORE

D0621297

SPANISH SLANGUAGE

A **FUN** VISUAL GUIDE TO SPANISH TERMS AND PHRASES BY MIKE ELLIS

GIBBS SMITH
TO ENRICH AND INSPIRE HUMANKIND

First Edition
17 16 15 14 13   5 4 3 2 1

Text © 2013 Mike Ellis
Illustrations © 2013 Rupert Bottenberg,
except illustrations of trumpet player on
page 49 © red rose/Shutterstock.com,
star on page 8, and spade on page 54.

Published by
Gibbs Smith
P.O. Box 667
Layton, Utah 84041

1.800.835.4993 orders
www.gibbs-smith.com

Designed by michelvrana.com
Printed and bound in Hong Kong
Gibbs Smith books are printed on paper produced
from sustainable PEFC-certified forest/controlled
wood source. Learn more at www.pefc.org.

Library of Congress Cataloging-in-Publication Data

Ellis, Mike, 1961–
  More Spanish slanguage : a fun visual guide
to Spanish terms and phrases / Mike Ellis.
— First Edition.
    pages cm
  ISBN 978-1-4236-3437-9
1. Spanish language—Conversation and phrase
books—English. 2. Spanish language—Textbooks
for foreign speakers—English. 3. Spanish
language—Terms and phrases—English. I. Title.
  PC4121.E624 2013
  468.3'421—dc23
                                        2013001326

CONTENTS

HOW TO USE THIS BOOK

If you have always wanted to learn the basics of Spanish, but traditional methods seemed overwhelming or intimidating, this book is for you! Just follow the directions below and soon you'll be able to say dozens of words and phrases in Spanish.

• Follow the illustrated prompts and say the phrase quickly and smoothly. Emphasize the words or syllables highlighted in red. A strikethrough means don't pronounce that letter.

• Learn to string together words or phrases to create many more phrases.

• Add "no" to the front or back of a phrase or make the phrase a question by inflecting your voice.

• The words and phrases are sorted alphabetically within each chapter to make finding them easier.

• Draw your own pictures to help with memorization and pronunciation.

Note: This book may produce Americanized Spanish.

For free sound bytes, visit slanguage.com.

VERBS

To accept
Aceptar

Ah Sup Tar

To answer
Contestar

Cone Taste Are

To be
Ser

Sarah

To come
Venir

Vein Ear

To commit *Cometer*	**Comb May Tear**
To contact *Contactar*	**Cone Tock Tar**
To cost *Costar*	**Co. Star**
To drink *Beber*	**Bay Bear**

8 VERBS

To eat
Comer

Comb Air

To enjoy
Gozar

Goes Are

To excuse
Disculpar

Dee School Par

To go
Ir

Ear

To happen
Suceder

Sue Say Dare

To have
Tener

10 Air

To jump
Saltar

Salt Tar

To kiss
Besar

Base Are

To measure
Medir

May Deer

To press
Pulsar

Pools Are

To say
Decir

Day Seer

To see
Ver

Very

To sleep
Dormir

Dorm Ear

To tell
Decir

Day Seer

To toast
Tostar

Toast Are

To vote
Votar

Vote Tar

PRONOUNS, PREPOSITIONS, AND CONJUNCTIONS

According to
Según

Say Goon

And
Y

E

As if
Como si

Comb Oh See

Because
Porque

Pour Kay

But
Sino

See No

Cone Toad Oh

Toe Doe Elm Moon Doe

Even so
Con todo

Everyone
Todo el mundo

Except
Salvo

Salvo

Far away from
Lejos de

Lay Hoes Day

For
Por

Pour

Him
Le

Lay

I
Yo

Yo

If
Si

See

It
Lo

Low

Like, as
Como

Comb Oh

Me
Mi

Me

Neither
Ni

Knee

Of
De

Day

Or, either
O

Oh

Otherwise
Si no

See No

Provided that *Con tal de que*	**Cone Tall Day Kay**
Since, from *Desde*	**Daze Day**
Something *Algo*	**All Go**
Than, that *Que*	**Kay**

That one
Ese

Essay

Unless
Salvo que

Salvo Kay

With
Con

Cone

With him
Consigo

Cone See Go

With you
Contigo

Cone Tee Go

Without
Sin

Seen

You
Tú

2

You and I
Tú y yo

2 E Yo

ADJECTIVES AND ADVERBS

All *Todo*	**Toe Doe**
Alone *Solo*	**Sew Low**
Also *También*	**Tom Bee An**
Better *Mejor*	**May Horn**

Blessed
Bendito

Ben Deed Toe

Comfortable
Cómodo

Comb Oh Doe

Delicious
Delicioso

Day Lee See Owes Oh

Difficult
Difícil

Dee Fee Seal

Dirty
Sucio

Sue See Oh

False
Falso

Fall Sew

Generous
Generoso

Jen Ed Oh Sew

Honest
Honesto

Owe Nest Oh

Hot
Caliente

Collie Yen Tay

Jealous
Celoso

Say Low Sew

Just
Justo

Whose Toe

Less
Menos

May Nose

Loyal
Fiel

Fee Yell

Magnificent
Magnífico

Mag Knee Fee Co.

New
Nuevo

New Wave Oh

Pretty
Bonito

Bone Knee Toe

Quiet
Quieto

Key Ate Toe

Ready
Listo

Lease Toe

Red-haired
Pelirrojo

Pel Lead Oh Hoe

Select
Selecto

Say Leck Toe

Skinny *Flaco*	**Flock Oh**
Slow *Lento*	**Len Toe**
Slowly *Despacio*	**Day Spa See Oh**
Small *Pequeño*	**Pay Kane Yo**

Smooth
Liso

Lee Sew

Solid
Sólido

Sew Lee Doe

Suitable
Apto

App Toe

Sweet
Dulce

Dual Say

Tall, high
Alto

All Toe

Very
Muy

Moo We

Well
Bien

Bee Yen

Wise
Juicioso

Who We See Oh Sew

Are you eating it?
¿Tú lo comes?

2 Low Comb Ace?

Do you know me?
¿Me conoces?

Me Cone Know Says?

From where?
¿De dónde?

Day Done Day?

How are they?
¿Cómo son?

Comb Oh Sewn?

Is everybody happy?
¿Estamos contentos?

Ace Tom Owes Cone 10 Toes?

What are you like?
¿Cómo eres?

Comb Oh Ed Ace?

What happened?
¿Qué pasó?

Kay Pa Sew?

What is . . . ?
¿Qué hay . . . ?

Kay Eye . . . ?

What is it like? *¿Cómo es?*	**Comb Oh Ace?**
What is this? *¿Qué es esto?*	**Kay Ace Ace Toe?**
What time is it? *¿Qué hora es?*	**Kay Odor Ace?**
Where is . . . ? *¿Dónde hay . . . ?*	**Done Day Eye . . . ?**

Which? | Koala?
¿Cuál?

Which ones? | Koala Ace?
¿Cuáles?

With whom? | Cone Key An?
¿Con quién?

You got it? | Low Tee Annies?
¿Lo tienes?

SPORTS AND ENTERTAINMENT

Baseball
Béisbol

Baseball

Biking
Ciclismo

Seek Lease Mo

Cinema
Cine

See Neigh

Concert
Concierto

Cone See Air Toe

Golf
Golf

Golf

Hockey
Hockey

Hoe Key

Jai alai
Jai alai

High a Lie

Marathon
Maratón

Mod a Tone

Mountain climbing
Alpinismo

Al Pee Knees Moe

Museum
Museo

Moose Say Oh

Musical
Musical

Moosey Call

Photo shoot
Sesión de fotos

Say See Own Day Foe Toes

Piano
Piano

Piano

Play
Jugar

Who Gar

Polo
Polo

Polo

Skin diving
Buceo

Boo Say Oh

Snowboard
Snowboard

Snowboard

Surfing
Surf

Surf

Tennis
Tenis

10 Niece

Track and field
Atletismo

At Lay Tease Mo

Triathlon
Triatlón

Tree Yacht Loan

Tuba
Tuba

Tuba

The voice
La voz

Love Owes

Xylophone
Xilófono

Ex See Low Phone Oh

MONEY AND SHOPPING

Cash
Efectivo

Effect Tee Vo

Do you have change?
¿Tiene cambio?

Tee Any Come Bee Oh?

Dress
Vestido

Vest Tee Doe

Expensive
Caro

Cod Oh

I need . . .
Necesito . . .

Neigh Say See Toe . . .

Is that all?
¿Algo más?

All Go Muss?

List
Lista

Least Ah

The market
El mercado

Elmer Cod Oh

On the fifth floor
En el quinto piso

Anal Keen Toe Pea Sew

The sale
La venta

Love Vein Tah

Shopping cart
Carrito

Cod Eat Toe

Biology
Biología

Bee Oh Low He Ah

Complex
Complejo

Come Play Hoe

Cultured
Culto

Cool Toe

Fluency
Fluidez

Flu We Daze

Gifted *Dotado*	**Doe Todd Oh**
Good grades *Buenas notas*	**Boo Wayne Us Note Us**
High school *Secundaria*	**Say Coon Dotty Ah**
Lesson *Lección*	**Lake See Own**

The newsletter
El boletín

Elbow Lay Teen

Notebook
Cuaderno

Koala Dare No

Two pencils
Dos lápices

Does Lop Pieces

| Bathtub | **Tina** |
| *Tina* | |

| Bed | **Comma** |
| *Cama* | |

| Bowls | **Toss Zone Ace** ♠ |
| *Tazones* | |

| Chair | **Seeya** |
| *Silla* | |

Dining room
Comedor

Comb May Door

The floor
El suelo

Else Way Low

Lawn
Césped

Say Spade

Mirror
Espejo

Ace Pay Hoe

Phone
Teléfono

Tell Lay Phone Oh

Soap
Jabón

Hop Bone

Sofa
Sofá

Sofa

Bear
Oso

Oh Sew

Cat
Gato

Got Toe

Goose
Ganso

Guns Oh

Lion
León

Lee Own

Mink
Visón

Vee Sewn

Monkey
Mono

Moe No

Mosquito
Mosquito

Moe Ski Toe

Owl
Búho

Boo Hoe

Pony
Poni

Rabbit
Conejo

Salmon
Salmón

Swan
Cisne

Pony

Cone Neigh Hoe

Sal Moan

Cease Neigh

Baggage
Equipaje

Achy Pa Hay

Copilot
Copiloto

Cope Pea Low Toe

Destination
Destino

Days Tee No

Map
Mapa

Mop Ah

Payment amount
Monto

Moan Toe

Pilot
Piloto

Pea Low Toe

Place
Sitio

See Tee Oh

The plane
El avión

El Lovey Own

Road
Camino

Come Me Know

Boo Kay

Ship
Buque

The suitcase
La maleta

Llama Late Ah

Traffic jam
Trancón

Trunk Own

Aspen
Álamo temblón

Alamo Tame Blown

Elm
Olmo

Old Moe

The fire
El fuego

Elf Way Go

Fish
Pez

Pays

Flax
Lino

Lee No

Gall oak
Quejigo

Kay He Go

Ice
Hielo

Yellow

Lavender
Espliego

Ace Plea Eggo

Lime tree
Tilo

Tee Low

Poplar
Álamo

Alamo

Reed
Carrizo

Cod Eat Sew

The sky
El cielo

Else See Yellow

Sun
Sol

Sole

Thyme
Tomillo

Toe Me Oh

Volcano
El volcán

Elf Vole Con

The world
El mundo

Elm Moon Doe

BODY PARTS

Ankle
Tobillo

Toe Bee Yo

Brain
Seso

Say Sew

Butt
Nalgas

Nail Gus

Elbow
Codo

Code Oh

Eye
Ojo

Oh Hoe

Face
Cara

Cod Ah

Finger
Dedo

Day Doe

Foot
Pie

P.A.

Hair	**Pay Low**
Pelo	
Head	**Cob Base Ah**
Cabeza	
Heel	**Tall Own**
Talón	
Lip	**Lobby Oh**
Labio	

Liver
Hígado

He God Oh

Lung
Pulmón

Pool Moan

The neck
El cuello

Elk Way Yo

Skeleton
Esqueleto

A
♠

Ace Kay Lay Toe

Skin
Piel

Pea Yell

Stomach
Estómago

Ace Toe Ma Go

Thigh
Muslo

Moose Low

Cloud
Nube

New Bay

Cyclone
Ciclón

See Clone

Downpour
Chaparrón

Chop Pod Own

Hot
Cálido

Call Lee Doe

Sunny
Soleado

Sew Lay Yacht Doe

It's sunny
Hay sol

Eye Sole

Thaw
Deshielo

Day See Yellow

Warm
Caluroso

Call Lude Oh Sew

SCIENCE AND TECHNOLOGY

Conducts
Conduce

Cone Due Say

Data
Datos

Dot Toes

Domain
Dominio

Doe Me Knee Oh

The icon
El icono

Elly Cone Oh

Internet connection
Conexión a Internet

Cone Neck See Own Ah Internet

Liquid
Líquido

Lee Key Doe

Modem
Módem

Mo Dame

Resolution
Resolución

Ray Sew Loose See Own

Sound
Sonido

Sew Knee Doe

Video
Video

Vee Day Oh

Web site
Sitio web

See Tee Oh Web

Baptism
Bautizmo

Bout Tease Moe

Confession
Confesión

Cone Fess See Own

Convent
Convento

Cone Vein Toe

Devil
Demonio

Day Moan Knee Oh

Devout *Devoto*	**Day Vote Toe**
God *Dios*	**Dee Owes**
Heaven *Cielo*	**See Yellow**
Jewish *Judío*	**Who Dee Oh**

Monk
Monje

Moan Hay

Pope
Papa

Papa

Pulpit
Púlpito

Pool Pea Toe

Saint
Santo

Sun Toe

Benefits
Beneficios

Bay Nay Fee See Owes

Bond
Bono

Bow No

Boss
Jefe

Hay Fay

Expense
Gasto

Gus Toe

Financial settlement
Finiquito

Fee Knee Key Toe

Fixed salary
Sueldo fijo

Sue Well Doe Fee Hoe

Judge
Juez

Who Ways

Mechanic
Mecánico

May Connie Co.

Miner
Minero

Mean Aid Oh

Partner
Socio

Sew See Oh

Salary
Sueldo

Sue Well Doe

Successful
Exitoso

Egg See Toe Sew

FOOD AND RESTAURANTS

Menu
Menú

The bill, please
La cuenta, por favor

Snacks
Antojitos

May New

Lock When Top, Pour

Fuñ Vore

Ant Toe He Toes

Cabbage
Col

Coal

Coconut
Coco

Cocoa

Corn
Maíz

My Ease

Cucumber
Pepino

Pay Pea No

Fried
Frito

Free Toe

Fried eggs
Huevos fritos

Wave Owes Free Toes

Ham
Jamón

Hum Own

Juice
Jugo

Who Go

Melon
Melón

May Loan

Noodles
Fideos

Fee Day Owes

Peach
Melocotón

Mellow Coat Tone

Prawns
Langostinos

Long Ghost Tee Nose

Pudding
Budín

Boo Dean

Sauce
Salsa

Salsa

Steak
Bistec

Bee Steak

Unsweetened
Sin azúcar

Seen Ah Zoo Car

SPANGLESE

All these words (and many more) are identical in spelling and meaning in English and Spanish. Although you may experience small slanguage pronunciation differences, you will still be understood.

- Alfalfa
- Alligator
- Anchovy
- Banana
- Barracuda
- Bravo
- Cabana
- Cafeteria
- Canoe
- Chihuahua
- Chili

- Cocoa
- Daiquiri
- Embargo
- Filibuster
- Hurricane
- Iguana
- Jeans
- Jerky
- Lasso
- Llama
- Macho

- Manatee
- Megabyte
- Mosquito
- Mustang
- Oregano
- Papaya
- Pimento
- Pizza
- Plaza
- Poncho
- Rodeo

- Savanna
- Savvy
- Silo
- Tango
- Tapioca
- Tobacco
- Tornado
- Tuna
- Vanilla
- Vigilante
- Yam